How To Ride Your **Unicycle**

A beginner's guide to the most ridiculous form of transport ever invented

By Charlie Dancey

Distributed by Unicycle.com

How To Ride Your **Unicycle**
Copyright © Charlie Dancey 1998, 2001
All rights reserved.

Published 1998 by Butterfingers, England. Revised and reprinted 2001

So stick a saddle on *that* and ride it.

The author cannot accept responsibility for people falling off things, especially when they know perfectly well that nobody can actually balance on a unicycle, it's just that some people have worked out how to take a *very* long time to fall off.

Fonts: ApCenter, Futura, Courier.

Software: QuarkXpress™, Adobe PhotoShop®, Adobe Illustrator®, MetaTools Infini-D™, Fractal Design Poser™.

Hardware: Macintosh.

Cover, illustrations, 3D modelling, words, layout, design and typesetting by Charlie Dancey.
charlie@dancey.net

A C.I.P. catalogue record for this title is available from the British Library.

ISBN 1-898591-18-0

Printed and Bound in Great Britain by The Cromwell Press, Trowbridge, Wiltshire

Contents

Introduction

Welcome!

The unicycle is, without doubt, the stupidest form of transport ever invented.

They have no steering, no brakes, hardly any frame, and it is quite impossible to park one against a kerb.

The unicycle was invented by mistake as a result of some serious technical problems with the Penny Farthing (see page 6) and it was a surprise to everybody when somebody discovered that you could actually *ride* one.

What's even more surprising is that *anybody* can learn to do this –even you!

They may be stupid, but they are good fun and there's something irresistibly appealing about adding to one's range of personal super-powers.

Some unicyclists are jugglers or performers who simply wanted to add another circus skill to their repertoire, but there are plenty of unicyclists who don't know one end of a beanbag from another.

There are keen cyclists who would feel they were missing out if they couldn't handle life on one wheel, and there are motocross riders keen to develop their balance skills. There are also people who want to do it simply "because it's there".

If you are a beginner, then get hold of a 'Standard Unicycle' (Page 8), set the saddle to the right height and get cracking. The younger you are, the faster you will learn. Unicycling is a physical skill, and no amount of *thinking* about it will help, all you need is practice.

Keep your sessions short, frequent, and most of all *fun*.

A week after you start, I guarantee, you will be amazed at your progress.

And finally, if you think this book is a little silly in places, I apologise. But I find myself unable to take unicycling *completely* seriously.

CHARLIE DANCEY BATH 1998

About Your Favourite Foot

You'll find a lot of references to your "favourite foot" in this book and I had better explain which one that is. It's your left foot. Unless, like me, you happen to be *right footed*. Which gets us precisely nowhere. So try this. Place a chair in front of you and climb onto it in one step. Which foot did you use?

Safety

Dressing Up and Falling Down

It might sound unlikely, but sensible unicyclists very rarely fall off. Instead, as the machine starts to get out of control, they *step off*, and ninety nine times out of a hundred, they end up completely upright and unharmed.

However, from time to time it all comes apart at the seams and before you know it you are eating pavement pie. It's therefore wise to take some sensible precautions to save wrists, knees, elbows, and that lovely head of yours from damage.

Skateboarders make it their business to fall off their vehicles with sickening frequency and they have mastered the art of not only escaping unscathed, but also looking very cool while they do it.

There's plenty of safety kit available for skateboarders in a range of colours that are loud and garish enough to satisfy even the most extrovert unicyclist and it might be a good idea to invest in some. If you're young enough to have parents who worry about your safety then you'll have no trouble getting them to chip in.

This is what parents are *for*.

Helmet, wrist protectors, knee and elbow pads are all worth having, especially if you are going to be working on hard ground.

Add to that some shoes that cover your ankles, to save you from the dreaded pedal-scrape and you are well-nigh invulnerable to minor falls and tumbles.

Where to unicycle

Ideally you should choose firm grass or smooth wooden floors, but if you have all that gear on, you could risk harder and meaner surfaces.

Make sure that the area is clear, stay away from furniture, people, dogs or badly parked unicycles. When it's time to step off the falling machine you don't want to be anywhere near *anything*.

Most importantly of all **avoid traffic**.

Car drivers have no idea how to treat a unicycle, they never give them enough room and worse than that, they get distracted by them and can end up hitting somebody else.

If you ride along the highway you take your life in your hands. So despite what the law of the land has to say about it (see page 31) you should consider yourself to be a pedestrian (and a pretty hopeless one at that).

Be safe, and have fun!

3

The History of One-Wheeled Vehicles

The unicycle was invented in the late 1800's when designers were still having serious problems making a bicycle that would actually go, stop, steer and get you from A to B faster than walking.

The 'Penny-Farthing' or 'Ordinary Bicycle'.

In 1869 they came up with the ridiculous 'Penny-Farthing' (also known as the 'Ordinary Bicycle'). This machine did indeed go, stop, steer and get you from A to B faster than walking, but it was also very difficult and dangerous to ride.

If you applied the brakes hard, or simply tried to prevent the machine from running away down a hill, the little rear wheel would lift off the ground. This almost always resulted in a nasty crash and over 1000 people were killed on these machines. Then, one day, somebody discovered that you could actually ride a penny-farthing on its front wheel *without* falling off.

Nobody is quite sure who first followed this idea through to its logical conclusion and sawed off most of the really useful bits of their bicycle, but that's what happened. And so, sometime around 1870, the unicycle was born.

Early Unicycle

Modern Unicycle

The early machines featured large wheels and had handlebars instead of saddles (because that's what you are left with when you chop up a Penny-Farthing). Over the years these would develop into the smaller-wheeled machines of today.

Meanwhile, people continued to fall off Penny-Farthings and kill themselves so cycle engineers went back to the drawing board to design a better machine. In 1887 this resulted in the 'Safety Bicycle' with its chain driven rear wheel and brakes that you could dare to use.

The 'Safety Bicycle'

The unicyclists and trick riders were quick to seize these machines and adapt them, creating 'artistic bicycles' that could be ridden in weird and wonderful ways, including backwards or on the back wheel alone. From there it was a short step to create the 'Giraffe Unicycle' which first appeared in the 1890's.

The boom years of unicycling and trick cycling were from 1880 to 1900 and during this time it was

The History of One-Wheeled Vehicles

discovered that even more ridiculous one-wheeled vehicles could be made and ridden.

The 'Ultimate Wheel'

By 1892 the 'Ultimate Wheel' had appeared. This is just a wheel with pedals attached and no frame at all! It looks impossible, but plenty of keen unicyclists have mastered them.

The 'Impossible Wheel'

The only one wheeled machine harder to ride than the Ultimate Wheel is the legendary 'Impossible

Wheel' (also known as the 'B.C. Wheel') which doesn't even have pedals, just two pegs for you to stand on. You ride these by setting them off on their own and then jumping on while they are going.

The 'Rim'

Remove the spokes and axle from the Impossible Wheel and you are left with a 'Rim', which is just a hoop that you roll along in. Kids have been doing this trick ever since there were hoops to roll along in. It's not so much difficult as dangerous.

Technically, the Rim is actually a 'Monocycle', not a Unicycle; a Monocycle being a single-wheeled vehicle in which the rider sits *inside* the wheel, rather than on top of it.

Pedal-powered monocycles were first ridden at about the same time as the Penny-Farthing and although many elegant machines were designed and built, they never really caught on.

Gauthier's Monocycle of 1877

Monocycles are very good for riding at a steady speed in a straight line and they are easy to balance, however they *hate* going around corners and if you slam the brakes on too hard you end up spinning head-over-heels like washing in a spin-drier.

5

Getting to know the Standard Unicycle

The Standard Unicycle is the right machine for the beginner.

Mechanically, there's not much to it. After all, this is a bicycle with most of the really *useful* bits removed. With so few working parts left, it follows that each of them must be very important. And so they are.

Saddle

The saddle is usually banana shaped, which is comfortable and easy to get a grip on. Some unicycles have posh little crash bars on the saddle which are good for getting a grip on, and protect against drop damage.

You should adjust the saddle height so that your leg is *almost* straight when the pedal is at the bottom. Note that you should place the pedal into the arch of your foot, only real experts ride on the tips of their toes and believe me, you are not an expert yet.

A unicycle *does* have a front and a back. and when you set up your machine, make sure that the saddle stem pinch bolt is at the back so you can tell which is which.

Set the seat height so that your leg is nearly straight with the pedal at the bottom.

Wheel

Most unicycles are fitted with BMX style fat-tyred wheels, which are good for riding on bumpy ground as well as being stronger than regular bicycle wheels. The wheel could be anything from 16 to 24 inches in diameter, with 20 inches being a popular choice.

Larger wheels make for a faster unicycle. Smaller wheels are better for Idling (staying on the spot). Speed isn't much of an issue with unicycling –the name of the game is *staying upright* rather than *going places.*

Getting to know the Standard Unicycle

Tyre

Your tyre will tend to wear quickly and in one particular spot, especially once you have learned to idle. From time to time you should let all the air out of the tyre, and turn it to a new position on the rim before re-inflating it. You can do this without removing the wheel from the frame.

Pedals

Pedals come in right and left handed versions. The right hand pedal screws into the right hand crank with a right hand thread and the left hand pedal contrariwise. You can tell which is which because they have little L's and R's stamped on them somewhere. The reason for this complication is that, on a bicycle, the normal pedalling action would tend to cause the left hand pedal to unscrew from its socket.

On a unicycle you tend to pedal in *both* directions. This means that unicycle pedals are more likely to come loose than bicycle pedals and you should check them for tightness often. Losing a pedal while you are riding is not a good idea.

Technical stuff

The biggest difference between a unicycle and a regular bike (ignoring obvious stuff like number of wheels, lack of brakes and so on) is the way that the pedals drive the wheel.

The pedal cranks are bolted directly to the wheel axle which turns with the wheel. On a regular bike the axle stays still while the wheel turns around it.

This means that a unicycle has an unusual bearing setup, with the bearings *outside* the wheel. This also means that you have an unusual type of wheel.

For 'unusual' read 'expensive'. You do not want to break your machine so check everything regularly; spokes, bolts, pedal tightness - the lot. Especially check that the bearings are securely tightened into the frame.

Your machine is ready to ride!

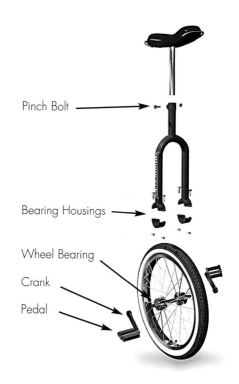

Pinch Bolt

Bearing Housings

Wheel Bearing

Crank

Pedal

First Wobbles

Getting On

Find something to hold onto. People are good because they giggle a lot, but they tend to get bored before you do, so find a handrail, or a fence or place two chairs back to back with a gap in between.

Get onto the saddle with the unicycle in front of you and place your favourite foot* on its pedal. The pedal must be right at the bottom.

Now say to yourself out loud, "**I will not take my weight off the bottom pedal.**"

You see, as long as you keep some weight on the bottom pedal, the unicycle will not scoot out from underneath you. This is the First Great Secret of Unicycling.

Now pull yourself upright, hanging on to your assistant, handrail or chairs, and put your other foot on the other pedal but **–do not take your weight off the bottom pedal**.

Sit there, relax, and try to feel comfortable.

Experiment with some little rocks, pedalling back and forth half a turn or so. Spend some time getting used to the feel of the unicycle underneath you.

At first it will feel like you are hanging on for grim death, but after a while you'll find you can actually sit on it. But whatever you do **–do not take your weight off the bottom pedal**.

*See page 2 if you're not sure which foot that is.

Getting off

Take your foot off the *top* pedal.

Do not take your weight off the bottom pedal.

Step forwards and onto the ground, grabbing the saddle with your hand to prevent the machine from falling over.

Now, and *only* now, you may take your weight off the bottom pedal.

It's a really *great* idea to keep some weight on that bottom pedal!

The Stepover

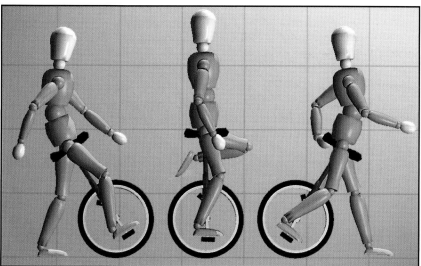

Place your favourite foot on its pedal and summon up a little courage...

Launch yourself forward and step right over the top pedal with your other foot.

As you reach the ground again, grab the back of saddle with the hand.

The Stepover

This exercise will save you a lot of trouble later on, because it teaches you the sensible way of getting off a unicycle.

The *silly* way is to crash in a heap of pedals, legs and spokes.

Get into the starting position, unicycle in front of you, favourite foot on its pedal and then practice stepping right *over* the unicycle with the other foot.

You don't need to hold onto anything to do this. Remember to keep your weight on the bottom pedal at all times.

This is how you get off a unicycle.

Practice this endlessly until it's second nature; that way you'll never need to go to the trouble of actually falling off.

While you are at it, get into the habit of holding the saddle as you step off; that way you'll save your machine a lot of knocks later on.

When you are quite sure that you have the stepover mastered, you are ready to 'Move About a Bit'.

Moving About a Bit

Moving About a Bit

Now that you know how to get on and off it's time to try a few wobbles.

You've probably worked out by now that the unicycle really is completely impossible to ride. It's as if your legs have been replaced by a sloppy meccano construction with most of the bolts missing. Whatever *you* want to do, the unicycle seems to want to do something else.

Usually that involves falling over.

Now it would be nice to be able to tell you some simple secret that made it all click into place, but sadly there isn't one.

It's all down to practice.

If you can find a handrail, so much the better. If not, then use the wall.

Get on the unicycle (by now you won't need reminding to keep some weight on the bottom pedal) and, while hanging on to your chosen means of support, see if you can wobble forwards half a pedal, so that the *other* foot is at the bottom.

OK, you haven't gone very far, but you've gone a *little way*.

In a couple of hours, apart from discovering several new muscles, you'll begin to feel much more confident about being on the unicycle and will be able to move around reasonably well –just as long as you have something to hold onto.

You may need to wobble around like this for a few days before the signals from your brain arrive at your legs in time to make any sense.

By then you should be able to make your way around a room using just one hand on the wall to steady yourself.

You've made major progress!

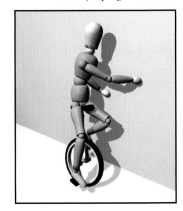

When you have managed all this you are ready to 'Launch into the Abyss'

Launching into the Abyss

Launching into the Abyss

It's time for the real thing now - actually riding the unicycle.

Choose a suitable large space to work in –paying particular attention to the floor which should be smooth and free of obstacles.

Start next to a wall and manoeuvre yourself onto the saddle. Turn away from the wall and launch yourself out into the *scary abyss*.

Aim to do two complete pedals (one complete revolution), before gracefully dismounting as you did in the 'Stepover'.

Keep working on this, and see if you can go from two to three pedals, from three to four, until you are making it as far as twenty feet from the wall before giving up.

Shout and wave your arms if you think it helps. It doesn't, but it makes you *feel* good.

Don't fall into the trap of trying to stay on like a suicidal rodeo rider. As soon as you feel yourself starting to fall, *step off*.

Don't try to go too fast, don't let it get out of control, and don't expect to get the whole thing sussed in a single afternoon.

An eight year old might manage a reasonable ride after only a couple of days practice, but anyone older than that could be stuck at this stage for a lot longer. Be patient, avoid hurting yourself and practice often.

Once you can cross the room you'll have a new problem –'Turning Corners'.

Turning Corners

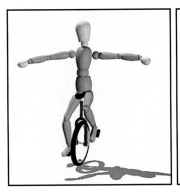

Learning to Make Turns

Once you start to make serious progress with 'Launching into the Abyss' you will encounter a new problem –the opposite wall! You have two choices. Either find an old airfield to practice on or learn how to turn corners.

Now it's pretty hard for the beginner to see how you can have *any* control over direction, there being no steering gear on the unicycle, but it *is* possible. Here's how.

Start by riding with your arms outstretched like aeroplane wings (as if you really were at that airfield).

Now swing your upper body around in the direction that you want to go in. Look in that direction too.

Push down hard on the inside pedal.

As if by magic, the unicycle will suddenly turn! Not only that, but it will also turn the way that you wanted it to!

Science is unable to explain how this works, but it does help you to miss that wall.

Practice turns to the right and the left, and do a few figures of eight for good measure! You should now start to feel like a real unicyclist,

ready to go out and explore the big wide world on your one-wheeled wonder.

In short –you can not only *go* places, but with your new steering skills you can actually go where you *want* to go!

Free Mounting

Starting position.

Launch forwards.

Step over the top pedal.

Hit the pedal, slam it back...

...and ride off!

Learning the Free Mount

The Free Mount is the technique of getting onto the unicycle *without* holding onto anything. This is useful skill to add once you have gained some control over what aircraft pilots call 'attitude' and 'heading'. Control over *attitude* means staying upright. Control over *heading* means going where you *want* to go.

To Free Mount your machine you should start in the same position as you did for the Stepover, that is, with the unicycle in front of you and your favourite foot on the bottom pedal, which should be pointing slightly towards you.

Now launch yourself forwards to bring the machine upright. Let your free foot curve through the air and slam backwards onto the top pedal, kicking it back a little as it does so.

This bit needs to be done positively.

When your foot hits the top pedal the kickback will push the wheel backwards for about a quarter of a turn which leaves you leaning forwards slightly and ready to ride off.

The kickback is important because without it you may end up with the pedals stalled in the dreaded 'top dead centre' position from which you will be unable to get any leverage.

If this happens you'll simply have to step off and try again.

The other thing to avoid is missing the top pedal altogether. It's funny to watch, but not for the rider.

The next lesson is 'Idling' –the art of staying on the spot.

13

Idling

About Idling

'Idling' (also known as 'Hovering' or 'Rocking') is the art of remaining balanced on your machine without actually *going* anywhere.

Believe me, this is useful.

It's not possible to balance the unicycle without moving at all, so to idle you rock the unicycle backwards and forwards over one spot. This means that you need to learn to ride backwards (which is tricky) but you only have to be able to ride backwards a tiny little bit (which is a lot easier).

The reason for all this rocking can be explained by some simple physics.

If you are balanced on one spot and you start to fall forwards, you can regain your balance by riding a little way forwards. And likewise, if you start to fall backwards you can ride a little way backwards to save the day.

But if you start to fall *sideways* you need to shuffle the unicycle sideways like somebody trying to zigzag their car into a tiny parking space.

And that's exactly what you do.

To idle you rock back and forwards over the same spot doing slightly under half a turn of the wheel from end to end of the rock. You'll find this an awful lot easier if you arrange matters so that your favourite foot is the one at the bottom. Here we see our unicycling hero doing a *right-footed* idle. This means that our multi-talented mannequin is probably right-footed. Either that, or he's trying to impress us with his ambipedal* skills. Really cool unicyclists learn to idle on *both* feet because it has the side effect of making them generally more stable when messing around on one wheel.

*Ambipedal = Ambidextrous, but for feet!

Idling

Learning to Idle

Idling is an advanced skill, so it's best to take it in stages.

Start your training by trying to do just one 'Rock'. Ride forwards normally, then come to a complete stop and go backwards for *just one pedal* (half a wheel revolution), and then ride off forwards again.

That's not too bad is it?

When that's feeling solid try doing *two* rocks before setting off again. That's backwards for one pedal, forwards one pedal, backwards one pedal again and finally forwards and away.

That's a little harder.

If you can manage three rocks then you are doing really well.

To make life easier you could park yourself in a doorway and rest the *backs* of your arms on the frame for some gentle support. Now idle that machine for all you are worth, as you improve you'll find that you need less and less pressure on the door frame to keep yourself upright.

Idling is a trick to be learned over a period of time. No amount of *thinking* about it is going to make it any easier, it simply has to become instinctive.

By combining doorway practice and short reversing manouevres while riding along you'll become an expert at idling before you know it.

Tyre Wear Warning

Idling causes extreme wear on your tyre, and in one particular spot. It's not unknown to see unicycle tyres worn all the way through to the inner tube.

The spot that loses its tread first is the spot that is in contact with the ground when your favourite foot is in the down position. Keep an eye on that wear.

When it starts to get bad you should deflate your tyre completely and rotate the outer tube on the wheel a quarter of a turn before re-inflating. You can do this without removing the wheel from the frame.

One of the best ways of learning to idle is to practice in a doorway using your arms to steady yourself, as time goes on you'll need less and less support. Mind you, the carpet might get worn out by the time you've mastered the trick.

15

Miscellaneous Mounts

The 'Side Mount' is just one of many ways to get on your machine. Here we are getting on by swinging our leg over the 'horses' rump. A variation is to swing the leg of the horses head instead. In either case you hang on to the saddle until the last

For the 'Suicide Mount' you start by plucking up courage...

...then leap!

With luck you will survive to ride away.

The Side Mount

This is a bit like getting on a horse. It's not much harder than a regular Free Mount but it looks pretty cool.

Stand to one side of the unicycle and place one foot on the nearest pedal. Then step on the pedal and swing your spare foot around the back of the machine before getting on and riding away.

You can make this harder (and a lot more dramatic) if you swing your foot around the *front* of the machine instead!

The Suicide mount

This is terrifying.

Stand the unicycle in front of you with the cranks in the horizontal position. Make sure the pedals themselves are also level.

Now just jump on.

You should make contact with the saddle and both pedals simultaneously. If you hesitate for a moment you risk a painful experience. It's not so much difficult, as just plain scary!

Miscellaneous Mounts

Kick Up Mount

This is a very flashy mount, but it's not that hard to learn.

Place the unicycle on the ground paying careful attention to the arrangement shown here. Your favourite foot goes onto the pedal and your other foot goes under the saddle.

In one smooth movement you transfer your weight onto the pedal, at the same time lifting the unicycle up with the other foot. Slam the saddle into your inside leg then sit down and get your top foot onto the pedal as quickly as you can.

There are quite a few things going on at once here, so you might like to make your first few attempts with somebody to hold onto.

The starting position seen from above. Favourite foot on pedal. Other foot under the saddle.

The 'Kick Up Mount'. Make sure you have the starting position right.

Now lift the saddle into position wile transferring your weight onto the pedal.

Once you are actually sitting on the unicycle, find the top pedal with your foot...

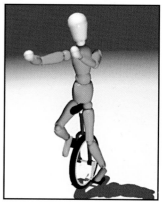

...and ride away!

17

Skillsome Things to Do

Picking things up

Imagine yourself to be a valiant Cossack displaying fine skills of horsemanship. See if you can bend all the way to the ground and pick up an object while riding past.

If you ever try to juggle on a unicycle, this will be a vital skill since you are going to be dropping those balls *all* the time.

Riding Backwards

If you have learned to idle then you can already ride backwards for at least one pedal. So why not go the whole hog and learn to travel backwards for a serious distance?

People are very impressed by backwards riding skills because here, at last, is something you cannot do on a bicycle!

The only really tricky bit is working out how to look over your shoulder as you go. Somehow the very act of craning your neck around seems to throw you off balance. This means it's a lot easier to go backwards *without* looking. This is not recommended for obvious reasons.

Bunny Hopping

Now this is easier than you think and a *very* useful trick to learn because it allows you to ride your machine up a kerb, or even up a staircase!

Get the cranks in a horizontal position and stand up on them, gripping the saddle between your legs (and holding on as well for good measure). You can now bounce the unicycle on its tyre, just like riding a Pogo Stick. It helps if your tyre is pumped up hard.

When you've mastered this, try riding up a kerb. Approach it as normal, then do one little *hop* over the obstruction, and carry on.

Skipping

With your **Bunny Hop** mastered you can now try to skip on a unicycle. You'll need to learn to grip that saddle with your legs only and it helps if you have one of those nice banana-shaped saddles on your machine.

More Skillsome Things to Do

Wheel Walking

This is a very skillful way of riding your machine. Instead of pedalling, you drive the machine by walking (backwards) on the top of the wheel, like a lumberjack rolling a floating log.

This is a five star skill.

To learn it, you'll need to find a handrail or something similar to lean on and then it's like going back to basic unicycle training.

When you are very confident you can try this without support.

Skilled wheel-walkers can ride along, hop their feet onto the wheel and walk it for a while before getting their feet back onto the pedals and riding off.

Wheel Braking and Gliding

A related skill is that of 'Wheel Braking'.

You build your unicycle up to speed, then place both feet on the wheel and use their braking force to control the unicycle as you slow down.

If you do this on the flat, then you can only brake for so long, before the unicycle comes to a halt and you'll either have to start pedalling, or wheel walking, to keep the machine upright.

But if you do it on a *hill* then it's a whole new ball game.

Let me tell you about one of the maddest things known to unicycle science.

It goes like this:

You get suited up with crash helmet, gloves, knee protection and full body armour. You place yourself on a unicycle at the top of a long steep hill. You set off and by judicious use of 'Wheel Braking' you glide down the hill.

Absolutely unheard of speeds have been achieved by this method, we are talking *over twenty five miles per hour!*

People really do this.

If you are mad enough to try then be warned that *you are going to fall off.*

It is therefore absolutely essential that you wear some very serious body protection.

Oh yes, and start on *little* hills.

Riding Positions from the Sublime to the Ridiculous

Correct Riding Position

Smooth and competent unicyclists learn to distribute their weight evenly between the pedals and the saddle and ride elegantly and in an upright position.

Bad Posture

Beginners often ride their unicycles as if they are suffering from severe back problems. This is obviously a *bad thing*. However, it's often used quite deliberately by performing unicyclists to make their antics look more comical and impressive.

One Foot

It's possible to idle with just one foot on its pedal. The 'spare' foot is usually tucked up on the frame.

Really skilled one-foot riders can travel forwards or backwards using just one foot.

On Stomach

Instead of sitting on the saddle, you lie your stomach on it and ride in that position.

It's bad posture taken to the extreme and can be very amusing.

Saddle to side

This is a don't-give-a-damn style of riding. The saddle is hooked around the outside of your thigh. It looks pretty painful but is easier to ride than you might think.

Holding Saddle

Instead of sitting on the saddle you hold it out in front.

The earliest unicycles had handlebars instead of saddles, so when you do this trick you are performing a piece of one-wheeled history.

Unicycling Games and Competitions

Unicyclists get together at unicycle and circus skills conventions, and whenever they do you can expect to see some pretty crazy games and competitions. See the Unicycling Contacts section (page 30) to find out more about the clubs and associations that put these events on.

Unicycle Jousting

Two unicyclists arm themselves with big padded lances and small shields. They stand off and then charge. Obviously whoever falls off is the loser. It's a great spectator sport.

This is supposed to be fun, rather than dangerous and it's therefore essential that the equipment used is carefully put together and *very* well padded.

Unicycle Hockey

This is taken pretty seriously. The game is very much like Ice Hockey, except that speeds are lower and people fall over a lot more.

Both England and Germany have a national leagues, perhaps more countries will follow soon.

Unicycle Gladiators

This game originated at Juggling Conventions, where 'gladiator' games are very popular. The rules of Gladiators are very simple, everyone assembles and starts doing whatever it is they do (unicycling, juggling or whatever) and the last person 'standing' so to speak, is the winner.

It's a severe test of nerve and skill.

21

Giraffe Unicycles

Here is the Second Great Secret of Unicycling: Promise that you won't tell.

Giraffe unicycles are actually *easier* to balance than ordinary unicycles; that is, once you can get on the things.

Think of it this way; if you try to balance a teaspoon on your finger it's a lot harder than trying to balance a broomstick. This is because tall things fall over more slowly than short ones.

And so it is with Giraffes.

Jugglers love them, after all, if you are trying to keep large numbers of flaming fire brands in the air while riding a unicycle, then you might as well choose one that is easy to balance. They also place you high above the heads of the crowd, which is good showmanship.

The height of a giraffe unicycle is measured like that of a horse (or the size of a TV screen) - that is to say, wildly inaccurately. They start at about five feet from ground to saddle, and this is a good beginner's choice because they are relatively easy to Free Mount. At seven feet it's still possible, but it's getting trickier.

From eight feet upwards you are almost certainly going to need a ladder. Machines of that height are really limited to procession and display work, rather than looning about on. They also become more dangerous.

Stepping off a five to seven foot machine is no big deal. Stepping off a ten footer is scary and painful (even if you get it right). Beyond ten feet you are in stunt person territory.

Some giraffes are fitted with double chains, one on each side, this is a nice feature, but not strictly necessary. The cleverly designed ones have slightly different sized chain sprockets, which completely eliminates the tyre wear problem of the standard unicycle.

Giraffe unicycles can be very expensive machines, far more expensive than a bicycle of similar quality. This is simply because they are produced in smaller numbers than bikes and so the cost savings that are possible with true mass production don't apply.

If you get one, get a good one. They take a lot of punishment and quality is worth paying for. The beginner should go for a five to six foot machine with a twenty to twenty four inch wheel and a fat tyre.

First Wobbles on your Giraffe

saddle with your favourite foot at the bottom. Now sit there and get familiar with the feeling of height. The first time you sit on a giraffe you will probably be reminded of the first time you swam in the *deep end*.

Experiment with a few rocks and get used to the increased weight of the machine. They are quite a bit heavier and more ponderous than standard unicycles.

Whatever you do, don't attempt to ride off until you have learned how to dismount safely.

Getting on for the first time

Make sure you are working in a clear space with absolutely nothing nasty to fall onto.

Also make sure that the seat height is correctly set and that all bolts are tight on your machine. Find some solid means of support that you can climb up and place yourself on the

Dismounting for the first time

The method of dismounting a giraffe is exactly as for the standard unicycle, except that you need to take it more seriously.

It's important to hang onto the saddle of the giraffe as you step off (because impact with the floor could easily bend your very expensive frame). This means that you'll hit the floor carrying the falling weight of the giraffe, so you'll hit it harder than you expect.

Put all your weight on the bottom pedal and

allow the giraffe to topple forwards like a tree being felled. As it nears the ground you can take your feet off the pedals so that you end up landing on both feet.

It's very important to practice this dismount until it feels perfectly easy. Once you've got it taped you'll never need to land in a heap.

Free Mounting a Five Foot Giraffe

This is the *only* way to get on your giraffe. If you fail to learn the Free Mount then you may as well carry a ladder around with you for the rest of your life.

Apart from being cool and useful, the Free Mount is actually *safer* than climbing up using a wall, lamp post or ladder. Safer because if anything *does* go wrong, you are falling in a clear area.

If your unicycle is a five footer and you can reach up onto the bottom pedal from the ground you can use the standard "foot on the pedal and Hup!" technique shown here.

Before attempting this, make sure you are confident about riding (and idling) on your giraffe, it's no good getting all the way to the top and then wondering what to do next!

Standing *very* close to the machine helps, because you are starting in a more balanced position.

Make yourself *believe* that you can do it, there's a considerable psychological barrier to overcome with this trick.

Start close to the giraffe with your favourite foot on the bottom pedal. When you launch up you need to keep weight on that pedal to prevent the giraffe from rolling away.

The moment of truth! get up as fast as possible and get your leg over that saddle. You should reach here with the machine still more or less in balance. If not, bail out, do a controlled dismount and try again.

Get onto the saddle, find that top pedal and kick it back hard, just like a regular Free Mount. That should leave you leaning forward slightly and ready to ride away.

Free Mounting a Seven Foot Giraffe

     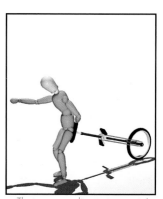

Jam the wheel with your foot. Lean the Uni slightly away from you.

Launch up and get your favourite foot onto its pedal.

Carry on up, time is pressing!

Get onto saddle and find the top pedal.

If things feel out of control then bail out gently.

That way you live to try again!

When trying to mount a seven foot giraffe (or any giraffe whose bottom pedal you can't reach from the ground) you have to climb up in two stages.

Start with your favourite foot on the *ground* and your favourite foot's pedal at the bottom. Step onto the back of the tyre with your other foot so that it jams against the frame. This foot locks the wheel and prevents it from turning.

Step up from the ground and get your favourite foot onto the bottom pedal. Now *that* foot is locking the wheel so your other foot is free to continue climbing.

From here it's much like the five foot mount, except that it takes longer. It's therefore more likely that by the time you have got to the saddle, the machine will be too far off balance for you to handle.

If that happens then bail out as shown here.

It's a good practice point to make it to the top every time, even if you can't stay up there.

Learning this trick is very tiring, not to say frustrating, so take it easy. You will get there in the end.

Whatever Next?

Ultimate Wheel

If you want to explore the outer limits of one-wheeled transport then you'll probably at least have a go at the 'Ultimate Wheel'.

This is the unicycle *without* frame or saddle, and at first glance the machine is clearly impossible to ride.

Most ultimate wheels are built with a wooden board in place of the spokes, the pedals are bolted directly to a piece of steel set into this board.

The secret of the ultimate wheel is that, with one pedal in the down position, and with the wheel resting against the rider's leg - the machine is *almost* stable.

By pedalling forwards once the rider reaches another *almost* stable position with the other foot down.

And that's how it's done. The machine is ridden forwards with the wheel flopping from side to side like a flapping fish's tail.

This can cause severe chafing to the rider's legs, so it's a good idea to get well padded up before trying it.

The Secret of the Ultimate Wheel. The wheel flops against the rider's leg which makes it *almost* stable, but also causes nasty friction burns. Notice that the design of the machine avoids the use of cranks, keeping the rider's weight close to the wheel and more on balance.

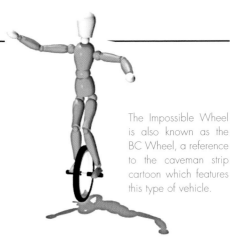

The Impossible Wheel is also known as the BC Wheel, a reference to the caveman strip cartoon which features this type of vehicle.

Impossible Wheel

As the name suggests, this is virtually impossible, but it has been done.

With no pedals, the machine cannot be *driven* but it can (by true experts) be *ridden*.

The wheel is sent rolling across the ground and then the rider Suicide Mounts the machine and controls it by means of careful Wheel Braking using the legs to pinch the tyre.

It's highly unlikely that you, dear reader, will ever manage this feat, but it's worth knowing just how far this one-wheeled madness can go.

Unicycles with too many Wheels

Eric the Half a Bike*

If you want to impress people then there's no need to resort to awesome displays of skill like the Ultimate or Impossible wheels. Sometimes the simple and easy stuff is just as effective.

If you can find the front end of an old bike, preferably with swept back handlebars rather than the straight kind, then you can push it along in front of you giving the illusion of riding a regular bike.

Then try hitting the audience with such amazing stunts as the ultimate wheelie, or negotiating traffic cones by sending the two ends of your pseudo-bike on opposite zigzags.

It's a definite crowd-pleaser!

Multi-Wheeled Unicycles

The machine shown here is a two-wheeled unicycle (which might sound like a contradiction in terms) and at first sight it looks like a clever design for a **Giraffe** with a friction drive to the lower wheel instead of a chain.

Simple to ride?

Think again.

The two wheels rotate in opposite directions, which means that the rider has to think *backwards* in order to stay aloft on the machine.

It's like learning to unicycle all over again.

It is, in fact, an awful lot easier (and more impressive) to ride a *three-wheeled* version of this –and plenty of unicyclists have done just that. There exists one amazing unicycle which is fitted with no less than *thirteen* wheels arranged like the workings of some insane clock.

It seems that there is just no end to the madness of unicyclists.

You won't believe this!

Unicycling Records

In 1934 Walter Nilsson crossed the USA on a unicycle. Nobody knows why.

Wally Watts rode one around the world in 1976 (got back home in '78), he did this to beat Walter. Pietro Biondo then rode the perimeter of North America (which is just as far, 12,000 miles) in 1983. He probably didn't like boats.

Ashrita Furman rode *backwards* for more than 53 miles in 1994. It sounds crazy until you realise that the forward-riding records were, by then, very hard to beat.

Curiously, unicycles don't seem to go that fast. The record (set by Floyd Beattie in 1988) is just 23mph over a 200 metre course. The high-speed gliding fanatics might have something to say about that!

The speed record for one hour's continuous riding is also set by Floyd at 15.88 mph. Surely somebody can do better than this?

Well, there's always Takayuki Koike of Japan, who did 100 miles at an average of 14.83mph. That's more like it!

And then there is the wild and wonderful Steve McPeak, who learned to unicycle to impress girls and then decided that the sky was literally the limit.

He rode a 32 foot high giraffe unicycle all the way from Chicago to Los Angeles (yes, that's Route 66). Pretty impressive stuff. Then, in 1980, he rode a 101 foot tall giraffe unicycle at Las Vegas (The Entertainment Capital of the World).

At the opposite end of the scale, Peter Rosendhal rode a unicycle with a 1 inch wheel for 12 feet in 1994.

In 1995, Duncan Castling and Simon Schofield, riding prototype MUni's* competed in the hideously tough Polaris Challenge - a UK event for mountain bikers that takes place over a gruelling course each year. They didn't actually win, but out of 564 teams they beat 176. And all that without gears or brakes. Curiously British law prohibits unicycles from using Bridleways so the competitors had to fix tiny extra wheels to their machines to compete in the 1996 event.

*Mountain Unicycles

Mad Unicycle Feats

Unicycles have been ridden:

Underwater
While bungee jumping
While abseiling down a building
While parachuting
On trampolines
Around both the North and South Pole
Down the Eiffel Tower
In aeroplanes
While wearing stilts
As daily commuter transport

Not only that, but Sem Abrahams (the legendary unicyclist who, it is claimed, has such an over-developed sense of balance that he is *incapable* fall off things) and his wife Teresa were actually married while riding unicycles. Most of those present were on unicycles too!

Tips for International Unicyclists*

Unicycles and the Law

According to the law, in most countries of the world, unicycles are not bicycles - so the sticky legal question is, do you ride on the road, or on the sidewalk?

It is a wise unicyclist who brushes up on the law before visiting a foreign country.

In England for example, a 'cycle' is defined as "a bicycle, tricycle, or cycle having four or more wheels, not being in any case a motor vehicle." As a result of the clumsy omission of the one-wheeler from this legislation, your unicycle is not covered at all by the Road Traffic laws and you can probably ride it wherever you like. Except, it turns out, on Bridleways which are for horses, pedestrians and bicycles (see opposite).

In California, interestingly enough, a unicyclist seems to be a 'pedestrian' which is defined as: "any person who is afoot or who is using a means of conveyance propelled by human power other than a bicycle". So unicyclists should stay on the sidewalk.

In New Zealand, a unicycle turns out to be a 'vehicle' which means that it can be legally ridden on the road as long as you give the proper hand signals when turning corners. It's not a good idea to push this argument too hard because as a 'vehicle' you are almost certainly required to have working brakes.

In Germany, the unicycle doesn't fall into the legal category of vehicle or pedestrian and in this country where people are sticklers for following the law this has left some of them wondering whether they can ride them *at all.*

They can of course, subject to the usual laws of gravity and indeed they do, in great numbers.

But not on the autobahn.

Sensible unicyclists smile politely at policemen and ride where it is safe to do so. Heavy traffic and unicycles go together like bulls and china shops.

Ride anywhere, have fun, but **avoid traffic!**

International Phrase Book

Here's how to say 'unicycle' in various countries around the world.

England	*unicycle*
Holland	*eenwieler*
France	*monocycle*
Germany	*einrad*
Japan	*ichirinsha or yunisaikuru*
Portugal	*monociclo*
Spain	*monociclo or uniciclo*
Sweden	*enhjuling*
Finland	*yksipyora*
Greece	*monopodeloto*
USA	*"Damn I'm good!"*

*Most of the information on this page was gleaned from the excellent unicycling FAQ on the Internet, and is reproduced here by kind permission.

Further Information

Around the World

The International Unicycling Federation
http://www.unicycling.org/iuf/

The Union of UK Unicyclists (U³)
2 Courtney Way, Kingswood, Bristol, BS15 9RB, UK
http://www.unicycle.org.uk

Unicycling Society of America
PO Box 40534, Redford, MI 48240 USA
http://www.unicycling.org/usa/index.html

The Australian Unicycle Society
PO Box 184, Lyneham ACT, Australia 2602
http://www.afmagic.com/fr_ausnews.html

In Print

Kaskade *(European Juggling Magazine)*
Schönbergstrasse 92
D-65199 Wiesbaden
Germany
tel +49 611 946 5142
fax +49 611 946 5143
kaskade@compuserve.com
http://www.kaskade.de

On the Internet

The Unicycle Page
All about unicycling.
http://www.unicycling.org

Steven Olderr's Bicyclopedia
An online encyclopædia of pedal-powered machines.
http://homepage.interaccess.com/~opcc/bc/

The Juggling Information Service
Unicycling help pages.
http://www.juggling.org/help/circus-arts/unicycling/

The Unicyclist's NewsGroup
Chat, discussion and questions answered.
rec.sport.unicycling

Contact Unicycle.com

For all your unicycle needs,
USA 1-800-UNICYCLE
http://www.unicycle.com
UK 0800 980 0711
http://www.unicycle.uk.com

Other Books by Charlie Dancey
Charlie Dancey's interests cover the whole spectrum
of circus skills.

The Encyclopædia of Ball Juggling
Why not add to your circus skills library with the galaxy's
greatest guide to gravity? 1500 tricks described with ruthless
clarity.
ISBN 1-898591-13-X
Published by Butterfingers

The Compendium of Club Juggling
Everything you could ever possibly need to know about club
juggling.
ISBN 1-898591-14-8
Published by Butterfingers

Contact Butterfingers

For more information on unicycle stockists, local clubs and
conventions,
tel 01647 441188
fax 01647 441185
mailbox@butterfingers.co.uk
http://www.butterfingers.co.uk